Stones
&
Bones

Stones
&
Bones

Char Matejovsky   Robaire Ream

POLEBRIDGE PRESS
Santa Rosa, California

www.stonesandbonesbook.com

Text copyright © 2007 by Char Matejovsky

Illustrations copyright © 2007 by Robaire Ream

ISBN 978-1-59815-004-9

First Polebridge Edition 2007

20 19 18 17 16 15 14 13 12 11 10 9 8 7 6 5 4 3 2 1

For additional resources, sheet music, and to learn more about performance and permissions, visit us online: **www.stonesandbonesbook.com**

See inside back cover for hidden treasure.

Evolution's the solution
to the data that we find,
when we study bones and fossils
and we keep an open mind.

Paleontologists, biologists,
and others A to Z
write the chapters of a story
that tells how we came to be.

In the rubble of a starburst some four billion years ago formed the kernel of a planet that became the earth we know.

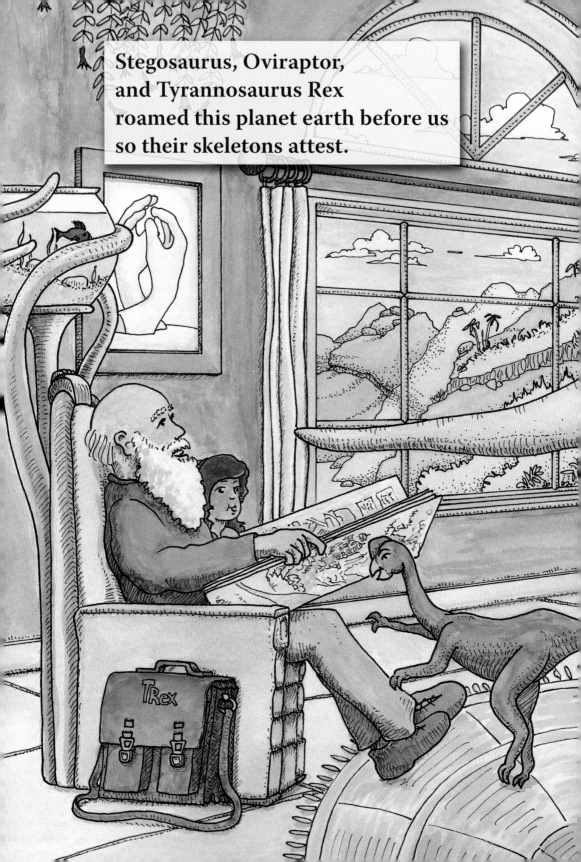

Stegosaurus, Oviraptor,
and Tyrannosaurus Rex
roamed this planet earth before us
so their skeletons attest.

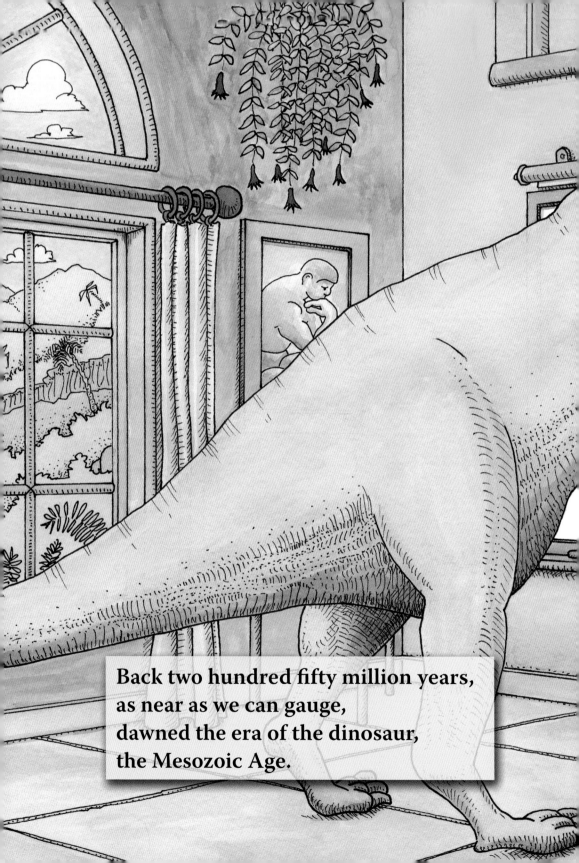

Back two hundred fifty million years,
as near as we can gauge,
dawned the era of the dinosaur,
the Mesozoic Age.

Through Triassic, and Jurassic, and Cretaceous days long past, they survived until an asteroid struck with a mighty blast.

About sixty million years ago,
no, make that sixty-five,
with the Cenozoic Age,
the age of mammals would arrive.

There were mastodons, and woolly
mammoths, platypuses, too,
and some big apes who one day would look
a lot like me and you.

From the Pliocene and Pleistocene
down to the modern age,
we find stones and bones and artifacts
to fill another page.

Some four million years ago, or so,
a quadruped stood tall,
started walking on its own two feet
and found it didn't fall.

And as time went by a biped
put its hand to making tools,
and soon many others followed
for, you see, they were not fools.

STONEHENGE

But Australopiths, Neandertals,
our cousins you might say,
who contrived to thrive for many years
cannot be found today.

Now the study of the DNA
in mitochondria
lets us trace our common mother
back to Eastern Africa.

Just a hundred thousand years, or two,
have passed, it seems the case,
since that very first appearance
of the modern human race.

Species sapiens of the genus homo,
yes, that means we're smart.
You can hear it in our language,
you can see it in our art.

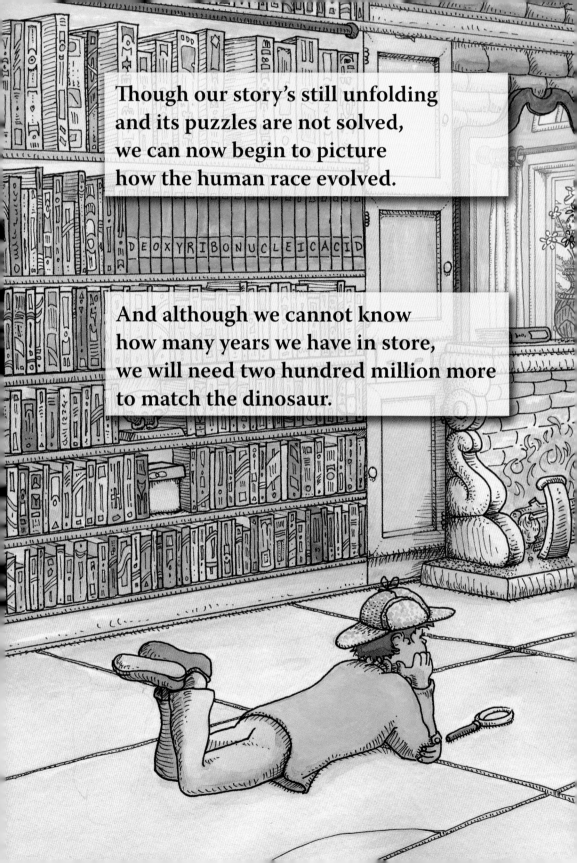

Though our story's still unfolding
and its puzzles are not solved,
we can now begin to picture
how the human race evolved.

DEOXYRIBONUCLEICACID

And although we cannot know
how many years we have in store,
we will need two hundred million more
to match the dinosaur.

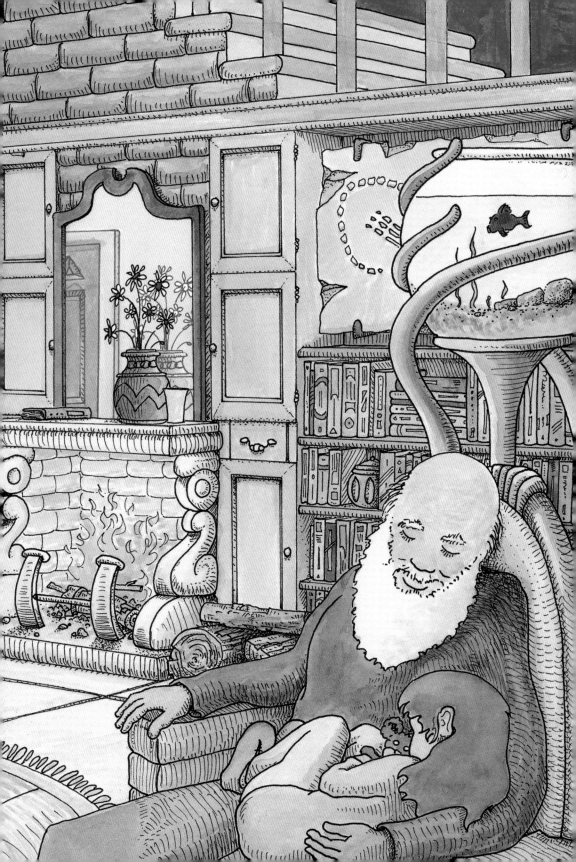

Australopith = Aw-**stray**-loh-pith

Cenozoic = See-nuh-**zoh**-ik

Cretaceous = Kri-**tay**-shuhss

Jurassic = Juu-**rass**-ik

Mesozoic = Me-zoh-**zoh**-ik

Mitochondria = My-tuh-**kon**-dri-uh

Neandertal = Ni-**an**-der-tahl

Paleontologist = Pay-li-on-**tol**-uh-jist

Pliocene = **Ply**-uh-seen

Pleistocene = **Ply**-stuh-seen

Quadruped = **Kwod**-ruu-ped

Triassic = Try-**ass**-ik